# DESIGN A LIFE YOU LOVE

---

## A Woman's Guide to Living
## a Happier and More Fulfilled Life

Michele Lamoureux

www.TheGoodLifeCoach.com

# Design A Life You Love

A Woman's Guide to Living a Happier and More Fulfilled Life

By Michele Lamoureux

Previously entitled, *The Goddess Guide: 52 Weeks of Inspiration for Living a Happier Life*. © Copyright Michele Lamoureux 2015. This book is a revised edition.

To contact the author, visit: www.thegoodlifecoach.com
Interior Book Design: Bruce Jones
Cover Design: Bruce Jones and Michele Lamoureux
Author Photo: Darren Pellegrino

ISBN-13: 978-0-9961967-0-3

Published by Lamoureux Media LLC

# Contents

Introduction   v

Chapter 1: Life   1

Chapter 2: Love   31

Chapter 3: Work   44

Chapter 4: Body   64

Chapter 5: Relationships   80

Chapter 6: Simplicity   99

Conclusion   121

Acknowledgments   123

*For Emma—my inspiration and love.*

# Introduction

Women tend to be in a constant state of doing—whether we are nurturing those we love or working hard to accomplish everything else that needs to get done. We often find it difficult to make time to explore our own desires and nurture ourselves. We get "busy" with life and the demands on our time. We end up feeling like we don't have a moment to reflect on whether we feel happy, fulfilled, successful, inspired and joyful in all areas of our lives. It is why I decided to write this book—to provide you with the structure and the space to think about what you want for your life. Every woman deserves to dream and to create a beautiful life—one that is a reflection of her deepest knowing—one that is in sync with her soul's truth.

There are 52 inspirations in this book. These inspirations are a reminder of how to design a life you love—as we are all the designers of our lives. We are part of the symphony of life—where we are both the artist and the canvas. As the designer of your life you have the opportunity to create the masterpiece that is your life. To do this, you need to have awareness about what you really desire, so that you can take directed action. I know from my own life that when I've been clear about what I most want, I am able to make positive change—like deciding to move my family across the country to California after living on the East Coast for over four decades.

I also know the pain of what life can bring—growing up wearing a back brace from the ages of ten to sixteen, which felt like living in a cage where I couldn't breathe. Not only did I lose a vital connection to my body for all of those years, but it also permanently reshaped my right side. What I've learned is that even the painful experiences in life give us the drive to make the changes we need for a better life. Our pain serves as a roadmap to redirect us to what is most important. This is why it is essential to own the parts of your life you have within your control and make it as abundant as you can dream!

This book is written for women because I believe that women need to spend more time thinking about what they really want from life and then take action on those desires. We are at a pivotal time in women's rights that requires more self-focus and self-love to create a new and brighter future for us all.

There are inspirations for every week of the year—spanning six categories: life, love, career, body, relationships, and simplicity. Life covers general philosophies about the areas in which you can live with more awareness and purpose. The chapter on love delves into how and why it is so important to always love yourself unconditionally. Career focuses on how to do work you love and to make the most out of your passions while supporting other women along the way. Body will teach you how to make treating your body a priority while appreciating all parts of yourself. The section on relationships reminds you to honor yourself and to choose whom you allow into your life consciously. Simplicity includes messages to inspire living in the moment to experience greater joy.

I hope that these inspirations will serve as your personal coach, walking you through each area of your life and offering insights, questions and calls to action for you to create awareness and positive change. Each inspiration includes a "Design a Life You Love Challenge" to further support you. The intention is to have you do the exercises in the areas of your life where you most want to experience change. When you have awareness about the patterns, responses and beliefs that you hold, you can take action. Awareness is the key to knowing yourself and living more consciously. Action becomes the small steps you take every day to design a life that reflects your desires.

The suggested ways to use this book:

1. Read it from beginning to end in the order that the inspirations are listed.

2. Pick a chapter that addresses the specific area you want to focus on, and spend more time on that chapter, knowing that as you take action in one area of your life, it creates positive change in all areas.

3. Randomly open the book and begin with the first inspiration you see.

4. Go through the 52 inspirations one week at a time. Also, find a journal that you love, so when you do the corresponding challenge you have a dedicated place to write your thoughts.

5. If you have a friend whom you believe would benefit from these inspirations, invite her to go through them with you. Having an accountability partner sets you both up for success. When you know someone is counting on you, you are more likely to show up and complete the task than you would on your own. It also takes the work you are doing to a deeper level, as you can reflect and share your thoughts and experiences.

6. If you would like more support and resources, please visit: www.thegoodlifecoach.com/book to download a free guide I created to help you live a happier and more fulfilled life.

In certain inspirations, I share client stories as examples of how small changes can make a profound impact for the better in your life. The names of the people have been changed to maintain their privacy.

We all lead very busy lives, which is why I chose to keep the format simple, concise, and easy to follow. I've purchased many "self-help" books over the years and often never found time to finish the book—as the busyness of life took over. Your time is precious. With this book, all you need is a few minutes to pick a page and to explore the concepts you most need to work on in your own life. The book is intended to benefit you, so use it in the way that feels best. I hope that it will encourage you to design a life YOU love!

# Chapter One

# Life

# 1

## Take responsibility for your life. You and only YOU are responsible for your happiness.

You are the one person you can count on for whatever it is you desire in your life. This is the good news and, for some people, the bad news. It is so empowering and important to take responsibility for what you want and need. When we lean on those we love, and look to others to validate our worth, we put ourselves in a situation that takes away our power.

You are capable and strong enough to manage your life. This doesn't mean that you can't ask others for help. A strong person does rely on others for support. A woman taking responsibility for her life seeks out the teachers, mentors, friends, doctors, and other resources that will help her live her healthiest and happiest life. But, it also means that you don't get stuck in a victim mentality. Many of us know someone who plays the victim. They are always at the center of some drama where they blame others for their problems. There are many ups and downs in life and knowing you have your own back is the first step to manage all that life will bring your way.

When you are honest about your contribution to your own life and can create awareness, you have the power to live life on your terms. You can find a job that really makes you happy. You can say "no" to a friend that doesn't respect your boundaries and attract new friends that do. If you want to start your own business, you can do the due diligence to get clear about the risks and benefits. You can register for the class or course that will empower you. If you are the type of person that takes care of everyone around you, you can choose to put yourself at the top of your list. Your life becomes full of opportunity and choice.

## DESIGN A LIFE YOU LOVE CHALLENGE

In your journal, write down the areas of your life that most need your attention—for example, relationships, health and finance. Rate your satisfaction in each area on a scale of 1-10, with one being the lowest and ten being the highest. For each area identify and write down what you need to do to take responsibility. Following are some questions to think about when journaling:

Do you feel taken for granted or invisible in your relationships or at work? If yes, what steps can you take today to be seen?

Do you attract partners that are emotionally unavailable? If yes, go deeper and ask yourself if there is a part of you that is afraid of commitment.

Do you have a supportive group of friends? If no, perhaps you are unintentionally keeping people at a distance.

Are there people in your life you can contact if you need help? If no, remember it is okay to lean on others at times. Let people close to you know that you would appreciate their support and let them know you are there for them too.

Do you regularly make time for activities that bring you joy? If no, why? Do you believe you deserve more joy? How can you begin to make time in your day for you own self-care?

Are you as healthy as you would like to be? If not, what needs to change? How can you make your health a priority?

Begin creating awareness around the patterns in your life. Do you see what role you have played in your life circumstances? What could you have done differently to feel empowered? Did you advocate for yourself, look to someone else to fix things or run from the situation? What steps can you take today to support your desires? By taking responsibility for your life, you will find more joy and peace.

# The opportunity for change lies in every moment.

There are times in our lives when we feel hopeless, frustrated or confused about next steps. It can be overwhelming. Remember that in every moment there's an opportunity to think, feel, and act upon the situation differently. When you shift how you're approaching a situation, it can bring about a sense of hope so that you can take action that's in your best interest. There is a wise saying by Albert Einstein, "We cannot solve our problems with the same thinking we used when we created them." How can you change how you are thinking about your situation to see opportunities you hadn't thought of before?

You can shift yourself out of a rut or procrastination at any moment. You don't have to wait for a new day, new week, new month or new year. The power of change lies within you at all times.

## DESIGN A LIFE YOU LOVE CHALLENGE

Do you have a situation in your life where you feel frustrated that you're not making any progress? Perhaps you've had one goal on your "to-do" list for longer than you care to admit. Ask yourself, "What is holding me back?" Once you have a better sense of the problem, you can make a plan to take action. Then, take one action step right now—for ex, make that call, sign up for a class, reach out to a mentor, or write your blog post.

Whatever it is that you want to accomplish, find an accountability partner. There is something very powerful that happens when you know that someone else is involved in your success. It becomes a great motivator, and one reason people hire coaches. Decide that this is the moment that you will put that change into action!

# 3

# Allow yourself to make mistakes.

Do you allow yourself to make mistakes or do you strive for perfection? Do you need to be in control at all times? Making mistakes in life is one of those things that we tend to avoid out of fear, but ultimately can serve as a great teacher. When we make mistakes, it means that we have taken action and are willing to take a risk. It means that we are engaged in life and willing to put ourselves out there. There is always something to learn from the mistakes we make, and it gives us a better perspective on life.

What if you accept that failing is part of the path to success? As we allow ourselves to make mistakes, we also give permission to those around us to do the same. We show by example that it is not about being perfect. It is about living fully.

When my client Amy wanted to start her own business, she was afraid of using public speaking to promote herself, even though she knew it was a great way to create awareness about her services. She had had an experience that she described as "humiliating" when she was giving a presentation to a large audience and forgot what she was going to say. What was a short moment of silence felt like an eternity to her, and she was afraid that it would happen again.

I had Amy take a step back and think about what she would feel if it had happened to someone else. She realized she would be supportive of the person, not judgmental. I also reminded her that an audience wants the speaker to succeed, not fail. She then shared how many members of the audience had come up to thank her for what they had learned. She had done a great job, even though she forgot what to say for a moment. To boost Amy's confidence, I suggested that she schedule a presentation for a small group of people. She set one up and it went great. By the end of the year, she was presenting regularly and her business was taking off.

### DESIGN A LIFE YOU LOVE CHALLENGE
In your journal, write down one goal or intention you have been meaning to act on, but haven't for fear of making a mistake. Ask yourself: "What is the worst thing that could happen? What am I afraid of?" Write down what thoughts come up for you. By taking some time to examine your fears, you will be able to address your concerns. By giving yourself the support you need, you will be able to take action.

Next, dedicate time every day to take small steps toward your goal. When you break down your goals into more manageable action steps, you will be less overwhelmed and more likely to move forward.

The truth is that even if we take the path of least resistance out of fear, we are going to make a mistake eventually. By realizing that our mistakes provide an opportunity for us to become more resilient, we can take more risks. We are also able to manage future mistakes with more grace.

# Turn your life into a trust fall.

Have you ever participated in a trust fall? A trust fall usually involves a team building exercise, where you stand up on a ladder and are asked to fall back into the arms of your co-workers, peers or friends, and trust that they'll catch you. It is a scary concept, as the alternative is that you hit the ground. Hmm, why would anyone do this? The truth is that it is exciting and freeing. It can feel good to let go and surrender and trust that all will be well.

There are going to be times in your life where you must surrender, to let go and trust that a higher power has your back. We are in the information age and tend to research and rationalize our way through life's challenges. However, once you have taken action, and things are truly out of your control, let yourself surrender to God, a higher power, universal consciousness or whatever you feel comfortable calling that force. Allow yourself to feel supported and to remember that you are never alone.

When we are in painful situations or trying to make change, it is easy to feel isolated and helpless in those situations. Take comfort in knowing that whatever you are experiencing, many others have, may or will experience as well. Everything in this universe is connected on an energetic level and you are not alone.

## DESIGN A LIFE YOU LOVE CHALLENGE

Write down what your desired outcome is for any situation that is troubling you. Take action where you can. Once you have done that, allow yourself to imagine some loving hands allowing you to rest back into them, and that all will be well.

# What you prioritize (not what you say is a priority) is what gets done.

Most of us have things we say are important to us, like our health, getting in shape, having fun, and time with family, but often our list of priorities is just that, a list. Much of it may be going to things that don't make us happy. Life is too precious to get locked into a routine that doesn't allow for your priorities. You may be wondering where each day went as you respond to all of the requests of your time each day. A sense that another day has gone and yet you are nowhere closer to the life you dream about.

### DESIGN A LIFE YOU LOVE CHALLENGE

Take a moment, get a piece of paper and a pen and make two columns. On the left column write a list of your top priorities and on the right, write down what you are actually prioritizing in your life.

The list of priorities could include things like: time with family, exercise, eating well, and meditation. On the list of where you actually spend your time, you may find that your list doesn't match. It may be filled with things such as errands, chores, family obligations, and doing work that you don't love.

The good news is that once you have your desired list of priorities, you can begin to make more room in your day for what is most important to you. Before you begin however, spend one week tracking how you currently spend your time. Be really detailed with this exercise. You may find that there are more pockets of available time than you realized. Here is an example of an action plan:

1. Schedule your priorities into your calendar at a time of day that is ideal for you. When you write it in your calendar, remember to make this time non-negotiable and be as specific as possible. For example, morning workout from 6:00-6:30 AM.

2. Evaluate which items on your list you can delegate. Then ask your spouse, children or someone you hire to help offset some of the things that take away your time. For example, if you can afford to hire someone to clean your house, you have now gained precious hours back in your day.

3. Get creative—when there isn't an option to delegate, can you make a game out of it with

your kids, so that you can enjoy family time while getting an errand done?

4. Learn to say "no" to things that don't require your involvement or feel more like an obligation than fun. This way you will have more time in your day for your priorities.

As we partner with ourselves and honor what we really need and desire, we can take action to live a life more aligned with our heart's desire.

# 6

# Be a conscious creator of your life.

Often we live our lives without taking conscious action to create a life we love. Time goes quickly, and by knowing what you want, you are more likely to manifest it. When you take the time to think about and write down what you desire, you become a conscious creator of your life. Knowing what you want for your life, and spending time each day towards those goals ultimately brings more happiness.

A client of mine, Carol, really wanted to get married and have children. But as she celebrated her 39th birthday, she was afraid that she had spent so many years focused on her career, that she had missed her opportunity. Our work centered around her making space in her heart and in her day for what she desired. She left work an hour earlier since she often worked late, changed the way she connected with others so that she was more present and open, and started to say "yes" to invitations. She also focused on being more loving and nurturing of herself.

She made space for fun and self-care. Within three months of her commitment to what she desired, she met the man that is now her husband and father of her two children.

What is the life you really desire? How does it match the life you are living? Do you dream of starting your own business? Moving to another state or country? Perhaps you have been meaning to workout regularly, but haven't found the time in your day?

### DESIGN A LIFE YOU LOVE CHALLENGE

1. Write a list of your desires in all key areas of your life.

2. Pick the top three desires on your list, in the order of their importance to you.

3. Make a plan to take action every day to make each of those desires a reality. Incorporate one desire at a time over the course of the next few months.

Nothing will change until you change. It is not only okay for you to make yourself a priority but essential for true happiness. Design a life that you love!

# 7

## It is okay to be afraid.

We all experience fear. We are hard-wired to react to situations that we perceive as being dangerous that trigger a "fight or flight" response. This makes us hyper-alert to a situation so we can determine if there is an actual threat. However, often it isn't an actual situation that has triggered a fear, but our minds playing out different scenarios of "what ifs" or gloom and doom thinking. So instead of being able to assess a situation, we can get stuck in a fearful loop in our minds. There may be past experiences or memories that heighten those fears within you. These internal worries may keep you stuck in a relationship or in a job that no longer serves you, for fear of making a change or disappointing someone else. Your fears can hold you back because you feel safer being invisible than having your full voice and self-expression. The truth is that our fears are also our teachers. As we pay attention to what frightens us, it serves as an opportunity to better understand ourselves and to have compassion for those parts of ourselves that need our love and attention.

## DESIGN A LIFE YOU LOVE CHALLENGE

The next time you feel scared, use it as an opportunity to assess what is going on in your life. Nurture that part of you that is afraid, the way you would a child. Ask yourself, "Is this fear valid or am I just afraid of the unknown?" Take some time to journal about your fear. Journal using these prompts: "I am afraid of" and "My biggest fear is." Write down whatever comes to you without judgment. By having a clearer sense of your fears you can take steps to manage them so that the fear doesn't overwhelm you.

For example, you may dream of moving somewhere new, but the idea of leaving what is familiar is too frightening. Go deeper and find out if this dream is something you really desire by writing a list of the pros and cons. Write down what excites you and what scares you about moving someplace new. Take time to meditate and see if your heart has any information for you. When we become too afraid to examine our fears, we can remain frozen. It is important to approach your fears with curiosity and compassion.

*8*

# Learn to make decisions.

Many of us lose precious time and energy worrying about "what ifs" and wishing something was different. Oftentimes we need to make important decisions—and it can be very overwhelming and stressful—especially if the decision impacts more than just you. So how do you take a complicated situation and make it not feel overwhelming?

**DESIGN A LIFE YOU LOVE CHALLENGE**
Go through these steps to help you with your situation.

1. Accept the situation for what it is. Acceptance is a powerful tool of surrender, and by surrendering you are allowing a higher power to work for you and your life.

2. Assess the situation. Ask yourself, "Do I need more information? Do I have resources that I haven't

explored yet? What is it that I need in order to make a decision?"

3. Take action when you are ready by committing to one small step. Make the phone call or go online and do the research that you need to help bring clarity to the situation.

4. Reach out to those who have had a similar experience and ask them for support.

5. Sometimes waiting is the best choice. If you are still unsure, don't feel the need to rush to an answer. Time may help clarify the situation.

# 9

## Your intuition is your trusted advisor.

We all have intuition, which is defined as "the ability to understand something immediately, without the need for conscious reasoning." Many of us have had experiences when we hear an internal voice or have a gut feeling telling us that something or someone is good or bad for us.

Sometimes women second-guess that inner knowing, their intuition. Moms can be looked down upon for trusting their intuition instead of logic when it comes to their children's wellbeing. Women entrepreneurs can be discouraged from taking risks when they have a gut feeling of something that could be the next big thing. The truth is that our intuition is a vital tool to guide us on our life's journey. Don't let anyone talk you out of what you know on an intuitive level. Learn how your intuition "speaks" to you, so you can discern when it is trying to give you information that is in your best interest.

Having worked closely with numerous CEOs, all self-made multimillionaires, one thing that I observed was that they all used their intuition. One CEO in particular would say, "I feel it in my bones" and often went against the industry "mind." He pioneered a niche before anyone else caught on that it was a hot market, and became known as a visionary in his field.

## DESIGN A LIFE YOU LOVE CHALLENGE

When in your life have you heard a voice or felt that gut feeling that something wasn't right? When have you felt something could be great and you should pursue it? Make a list of those times and write about how they turned out for you, so you have a better sense of how your intuition has served you in the past. When we get connected to our intuition, we get connected to our higher self and have a stronger connection to our life's purpose.

# *10*

## If you can tell yourself the truth,
## your life can unfold.

Do you have passions and dreams that you never share with anyone? Do these ideas that seem so big come into your heart and consciousness, but you push them aside because they seem unattainable? What would happen if you allowed yourself to dream? What would happen if you spoke your truth?

There are times when we find ourselves in relationships, jobs, living situations, or whatever it may be, that aren't working. We try to make them work and stay the course, but inside, our heart is breaking, and we don't know how to set ourselves free. Freedom comes from being honest with yourself. You don't have to announce to everyone what you are really feeling, but you do need to acknowledge it within. When we own our truth, we open the door to possibilities. It is in that place of truth that magic can happen.

**DESIGN A LIFE YOU LOVE CHALLENGE**
Journal without judgment to connect to what is true for
you in your life. Following are some sample questions
that you can ask yourself.

- Do you love your work? If not, what would you be
  doing if you could manifest anything you desire?
  If money didn't matter, what would you do for
  free?

- Are you happy with your relationships? If not,
  what needs to change?

- Do you have a connection with something higher
  than yourself? If not, why? How important is that
  to you?

- Do you love your home? How can you make it
  reflect more of the real you?

- How do you treat your body? Do you nourish it
  with healthy foods that make you feel great? Do
  you make time to stay fit? If not, what steps do
  you want to take to make a positive change?

# 11

## Life is about remembering.

As I sat journaling one day, the words "life is about remembering" came to me. I sat and really thought about this message. Remembering? Remembering what?

Life is about remembering who we are at a soul level. It is about remembering to choose love and to act out of love. Life is about remembering to evolve our capacity for love and to remember that love heals everything. It is about paying attention to those voices inside that make you feel like you want to do more with your life, that you are, in fact, meant to do more with your life.

So many of us are afraid to put ourselves out there. We do jobs that are convenient or safe. We hide behind our partners. We don't speak our truths. It's time to allow ourselves to daydream about the things that make us happy. Remembering who we are is part of our soul's journey.

## Design a Life You Love Challenge

Set aside at least 15 minutes to journal. During this dedicated time, write on the top of the page "Life is about remembering." Then, without stopping, allow yourself to write down all of the things that come to you. Next write on the top of another page "I remember" and write down all of the things you remember about yourself. For instance, that voice that says, "I remember how happy I am when I paint." Think about the things that excited you and brought you joy as a child. Allow this time to reconnect you to the themes in your life and to incorporate some of these activities again. Whatever it may be, create a space for that inner remembering to unfold.

# *12*

# Make pleasure a priority in your life.

Women are natural nurturers and when someone we love is in need, we want to be there to help in anyway we can. However, often our desire to help those we love can take away from our well-being.

Many women have told me they feel "guilty" for putting themselves first. A definition of guilty is "responsibility for a crime or for doing something bad or wrong." This sense of guilt can come from even simple things like taking time for a massage, enjoying a cup of coffee alone, or for buying something more expensive than you would normally spend on yourself. Why do acts of pleasure equate to feeling like we have done something criminal? Why do we mentally punish ourselves for wanting to feel good?

What if we could make pleasure a normal part of our being? Seems reasonable to believe that practicing self-care more often would actually be the opposite of doing something bad or wrong. If we are going to stand in our power, we need to feel worthy of not just loving others, but loving ourselves.

### DESIGN A LIFE YOU LOVE CHALLENGE

What if you started your day thinking about what would bring you pleasure? What would your day look like? How would you choose to spend your time?

Write a list of all of the things that make you happy. Keep adding to it as you think of things and incorporate some form of pleasure into your life every day!

# *13*

## Life is a gift and so are you.

Every day is a gift—an opportunity to move closer to being your truest self. Isn't it amazing how we get to wake up every morning and begin our day however we choose? Sure, we can let the day unfold and follow the same routines that keep creating the life situations that we complain about, or, we can begin to see the gift of opportunity that each day holds. We can choose to remember that we have been given this one precious life—a life that is inviting us to live fully and to come play.

It isn't easy to stay present to the miracle of our existence or to believe that we here for a reason. However, you can take time every day to notice and appreciate the beauty that surrounds you as a way of reconnecting to life—and to yourself. It doesn't need to take long. It is about coming back to the moment and to notice the gifts that surround you.

Babies are a great reminder of the gift of life. They come into this world embodying their full selves—open to love —open to learning—open to growing. The pets in our life offer joy in their very being—their ability to be in the moment and love you. The graceful trees and flowers surround you with beauty, while the ocean and waves dance and play a rhythmic beat, much like the way your heart beats its own song. Do you see how life is inviting you to see the magic that surrounds you and that is you? It is greeting you every day, in many ways, and reminding you that it loves you.

**DESIGN A LIFE YOU LOVE CHALLENGE**
Take a moment to center yourself by taking a few relaxing deep breaths. Put your hand on your heart and allow yourself to be grateful for the gift of life. Write down the many ways that life is inviting you to be a part of it.

Think about whether having a connection to God, a higher power or universal consciousness is important to you. If so, make time to connect with God (whatever you call that force in your life) regularly. When we remember that we are not alone, it gives us comfort and courage to live a fuller life.

# Chapter Two

# Love

## *14*

# Begin with yourself and everything else will fall into place.

Whatever it is you desire in life, it needs to start with you. If you want more joy, give yourself that joy. Spend time in nature; buy yourself flowers; wear clothes that make you feel great; take a course that inspires your creativity.

If you want better relationships, start with yourself. Treat yourself the way you want others to treat you. Talk to yourself with only love and kindness. You will find that when you give yourself what you deserve, instead of waiting for others, your life can unfold in beautiful ways that you never imagined. You will have a better relationship with yourself and attract equally loving ones into your life. You may even find some relationships go away because they no longer serve you.

When you love yourself, you make decisions that support your best interest. You eat well, exercise, make time for meaningful relationships and do work that you love. The idea is to look to yourself first to create the life you want.

When my client Katie wanted more attention from her husband, I suggested that she first work on giving herself the attention she was missing. She started to make time for herself every morning by getting up thirty minutes earlier than her family. She spent some time meditating and journaling so she could stay connected to what she was feeling and enjoyed a cup of tea in solitude. She felt more in control of her mornings and began to feel happier. After just a few weeks of this new practice, her husband started to ask her more questions about her life and asked if they could schedule a long overdue date night.

## DESIGN A LIFE YOU LOVE CHALLENGE
Write down one thing that you want or need that you have been looking outside of yourself to obtain. Make a plan—at that moment—to fulfill that desire or need. By giving yourself the love, time and opportunity to have what you want, you create the ability to bring it into your life.

## *15*

# Invite love into all areas of your life.

Love is one of the most powerful emotions we can feel. It is a driving force in all areas of our life. When we can bring love into our relationships, not only with our family and friends, we can shift people's energy to a more positive state.

When we turn on the news, it is mostly filled with what feels like the opposite of love, with very few stories that are about the goodness in people. Messages of violence and corruption, and basically anything that generates fear is what dominates. Even the weather can be presented with negatives messages to "watch out" and "be careful." There are very few stories on the presence of love, if any at all.

The majority of people are good at heart. There are billions of people on this planet that we share. Most people desire a happy and peaceful life, and a future that is better for their children than it was for them. Wouldn't it be great if what we took in every day were about all of the positive things happening in the world? How would we feel about one another? Isn't it likely that there would be less fear and violence as a result? Wouldn't it be nice to tune into stories of hope, connectedness and faith every day?

## Design a Life You Love Challenge

Ask yourself how you can bring more love into your life and to the lives of others every day. Write down a list of the areas of your life that need more love. Next to each area, write down things you can do to invite in love. As we are able to connect from a place of love within ourselves, we are able to resonate on a higher frequency. Our willingness to act out of love will inspire others to do the same. We are able to remember that we are all really one.

# *16*

# Love yourself unconditionally no matter what is happening in your life.

D o you love yourself? I mean really, truly love yourself? Do you talk kindly and treat yourself like a Goddess? Do you do things that honor you at all times? If not, why?

When we are in relationship with others we can focus on their needs instead of our own. We may forget to cherish our desires. When we take the time to love and honor our needs, we feel taken care of and fulfilled. We aren't waiting for others to make us feel whole. Our life unfolds in beautiful ways and the world around us begins to reflect the world within us.

What would your life look like if you loved yourself unconditionally? It wouldn't matter if you made mistakes, failed, or were completely lost. You would love yourself just the same, here in this moment, and that would be enough.

## DESIGN A LIFE YOU LOVE CHALLENGE

Think about any situation going on in your life where you hear those harsh voices in your mind criticizing you. Perhaps it is someone else saying things to you to make you feel less than you are? Use self-love to heal yourself and this situation. If you were talking to a friend, what would you say to make that person feel better? What would you encourage your friend to do? Do the same for yourself.

Take some time to practice loving affirmations. An affirmation is a positive statement made in the present tense that asserts a situation is true right now. Every day say out loud, "I love myself just as I am."

Write a list of the things that make you feel loved and do them for yourself. For example, you can prepare delicious, healthy meals to nourish your body—which you sit down to savor and enjoy with family and friends. Surround yourself with people that make you happy.

# 17

## See yourself from your own eyes (not your mother's, father's, partner's, friend's, family's) and cherish what you see.

When we are born, we are vulnerable beings welcomed into this world by the people around us. Our early memories of ourselves are created by how we were spoken to and treated from the time we were born. How much emotional stimulation, validation, smiles, attention and other interactions all impacted how much love we felt. Any messaging we received about our body, how we look, how we act, are all tied together to create our perceptions of our value in this world.

As we get older, we try to separate from the labels that were put on us as children. This can be a very painful and hard exercise to do, as we may fear that we will lose the love of those we hold close. In spite of any fear of separation, it is essential that we start seeing our true selves. The people who put labels on us may have done so out of their own fear and need to be in control. Or maybe they did it out of good intentions. Either way it shaped how we saw and felt about ourselves.

## DESIGN A LIFE YOU LOVE CHALLENGE

Write down the labels that people put on you—such as, "you're so: loud, fat, skinny, tall, short, stupid, picky, stubborn, bossy, or competitive." The idea is to identify the words that left you feeling criticized, shamed or different. The labels that made you believe that you weren't good enough just as you are. No one has the right to tell you who you are and what you are all about. Take some time to write your story—with you as the heroine—a story that describes the real you. Next, create a personal mission statement using descriptive words that resonate with you. Place it where you can see it every day to reinforce your sense of self.

Next time you have internal thoughts with those old labels, affirm to yourself that you are lovable and perfect the way that you are. Remember the heroine that lives within you. Whatever your early experiences were, you now have an opportunity to be that supportive parent that you may have needed for yourself. All that matters now is that YOU see YOU and that you give yourself the love you deserve.

# *18*

## Children are our teachers.
## They remind us to love life.

hildren are the greatest gift. They show up as these very wise, loving souls, with their distinct personalities intact, yet they are vulnerable and need us to survive. It is their vulnerability that ignites our own and helps us to grow as people.

Children approach life with curiosity and a desire to play while maintaining their focus in the moment. They love life and know that happiness is their birthright. Do you still live your life in this way? Do you want to feel the joy of being a child again?

### DESIGN A LIFE YOU LOVE CHALLENGE
Live your life from a child's perspective. When you wake up, focus on the attributes of curiosity and play, and practice being in the moment. Here are some ways to incorporate these concepts into your life:

1. Be curious.

   The curiosity of a child is insatiable. They study and inquire daily, even when they can't talk. When is the last time you learned something new or went deeper into a topic of interest to you? Write down one thing you would like to learn more about and make time to focus on it this week.

2. Play more often.

   Children seek out play from the moment they wake up. What about you? Is play a focus of your day? What is one fun thing you can do for yourself today? What would make your inner child happy? For example, you can sign up for an improv class to experience more laughter and joy.

3. Be present.

   Children are fully engaged in whatever it is they are doing. It can be challenging as an adult to keep the level of focus a child has when we join them in an activity. If you notice yourself thinking about the next thing on your "to-do" list, or stressing about something, bring yourself back to the moment. Use your breath as a way to remain present. Breathe in and out slowly a few times until your mind has relaxed and you can focus on what is in front of you. The more times you are able to stop yourself from thinking about the past or focusing on the future, the more joy you will experience.

# *19*

# Be your own best friend and champion.

Being your own best friend and champion is about remembering that you are worthy of your own love, and love in general. It is about comforting, supporting, and guiding yourself in a way that you would a dear friend or someone you love.

We all want to be loved and appreciated for our unique contributions, but if we wait for others to validate us, we can feel invisible or undervalued.

We may have dreams at some point in our life, whether they are little or big. When we share those ideas, there are always people, even people that we love like family, who may not see our vision as clearly as we do. Instead of being supportive, they may instill fear and doubt. Others may criticize or reject a dream that we hold dear to our hearts, which is often why many people don't share their dreams or follow through on them.

We all want to achieve things in life. Start with being your number one fan, and see how that supports the action you need to create a life you love.

## DESIGN A LIFE YOU LOVE CHALLENGE
If you fall, pick yourself back up and give yourself a hug. If you fail, tell yourself there's always another opportunity to try again. If your heart gets broken, love yourself the way that you want to be loved by others. Be your own best friend and heroine. We are often kinder to others than we are to ourselves. It is time to change that pattern by championing you.

Chapter Three

# Work

# *20*

You have a gift that is UNIQUELY yours. It is that something special that comes easily to you and brings you joy.

Do you have a feeling that you are here for something bigger than what you are doing now? Do you allow yourself to pursue that feeling and to follow that path? We are all born with a special gift that we are meant to bring to this planet. Your gift is that special something that comes easily to you, and when you are engaged in that activity you lose track of time. It also brings you great joy. You deserve to do work that you love.

**DESIGN A LIFE YOU LOVE CHALLENGE**
Here are some questions to think and journal about to become aware of your unique gifts. See if any patterns emerge. Allow yourself to dream and know it is okay to desire more. Once you become more clear, begin exploring ways that you can incorporate your special gift.

45

- What are your strengths?

- What activities do you do where you lose all track of time because you are so immersed in a positive way?

- Ask the people who know you best what they see as your unique talents.

- What secret desire do you have professionally that you are afraid to talk about—that one thing you dream of but never think could become a reality?

- When you were a child, what did you dream of doing when you grew up?

- If money weren't an issue, what would you be doing instead of your current work?

- What questions/problems do people you know commonly ask you to help solve?

# *21*

## Embrace your femininity.

Women in corporate America can lose their femininity as they compete for better positions and pay. This is not meant to be a criticism of a fellow sister—women historically have had to work harder than younger women do now to get to the level of power they have earned. However, when a woman can retain her femininity—that is a woman truly owning her power. A woman who embodies her femininity is able to express her intelligence and worth on her terms. She is able to model what is possible for other women. She teaches others what her boundaries are and professionally handles any missteps of those boundaries to change the situation or even the culture of a company. Our femininity has a place everywhere we go, whether it is at work, in relationships, or in parenting. Embrace that part of you in every environment and know that all things in life need balance.

There are many derogatory phrases that connect something feminine to weakness. A good example is a commercial that played during the 2015 Super Bowl. The producers of the brand *Always*® ran an advertisement that showed the negative associations connected to the phrases "run like a girl" and "throw like a girl," among others. The commercial demonstrates how adults—both men and women—see these messages as being less than, but when they asked little girls, they saw it for what it meant, just being themselves, which is fast and capable. Let's own our femininity. Being feminine is being powerful.

**DESIGN A LIFE YOU LOVE CHALLENGE**
What does the word "feminine" mean to you? Write down your own definition, as each woman needs to know what it means to her. Do you feel that you can express your femininity at work? Do you find that some men treat you differently at work because you are a woman? What about other women in the workplace? The more awareness we have, the better chance we have at making positive changes in our work environments.

Think about how you embrace your femininity. Do you feel like you can be feminine in certain areas of your life but not in others? Why not? Practice being your feminine self in every area of your life.

If someone uses a phrase that reinforces negative stereotypes of girls or women, speak up. Educate those around you.

## 22

# Support other women in business.

Women in business need to be supportive of one another. Many women see other women as competition and are harder on them than they are to men. If we want equal pay and better advancement opportunities, we need to support one another. There are already enough barriers created by many men in the business world that limit a woman's ability to get the job and pay they deserve. Certain company cultures—especially in finance—have a reputation of holding women back. This is why it is even more important for women to come together to take a stand. This is not to say that a woman should promote a woman over a man if the man is more qualified for the job. It is about not overlooking the qualified woman because she is perceived as a threat. The good news is that there are many strong women in business who really support other qualified women.

The truth is that women in business are an asset. In *ThinkAdvisor.com*, September 29, 2014, they write, "More and more research shows that increasing the number of female employees you have will boost your firm's bottom line."

### DESIGN A LIFE YOU LOVE CHALLENGE

Think about how the men and women in your office treat women. Is it a positive atmosphere for women, not just at the entry level, but also as you climb higher up into the C-level positions? Do the men support women's advancement? If not, can you form a women's group to create positive change for the women in your company? Can you enlist the support of other men? If you don't bring attention to an issue, it often stays the same or can get worse.

Think about what role you play in support of women in your office. Do you have a positive mentor in your life? Are there women you would like to mentor? Having a mentor to model can be very powerful at any stage in your career. If you don't have a personal mentor, there are books, podcasts, workshops and conferences that provide opportunities for you to grow professionally and personally.

# 23

## Your ideas are your own.

Many of us have had the experience of having our ideas claimed by someone else as their own. It feels really lousy doesn't it? Well, it's not okay.

Jen shared how her boss took an idea Jen had proposed and presented it as her own to the CEO of the company. The CEO loved the idea, which made Jen feel good but also angry at the same time, as she wasn't given any recognition. She wanted to say something to her boss but didn't know how. The first time it happened, Jen figured it was unintentional. However, as time went on, Jen realized that this was a pattern of deliberately taking Jen's ideas without attribution. We discussed how even if Jen didn't feel comfortable saying anything in front of the CEO, she could have addressed it with her boss later. Jen could let her know that it wasn't okay to take her ideas, as she would like to be acknowledged for them. If you are brainstorming and are okay with sharing your ideas without credit, that is fine, but if you aren't, there needs to be clear boundaries.

## DESIGN A LIFE YOU LOVE CHALLENGE

If you are in a position where someone else is intentionally claiming your ideas, first acknowledge their value to you. Evaluate your situation and determine how you can speak up for yourself. For example, if someone tries to take ownership of something you just said, say something like "I'm glad that my idea resonated. I think that the following would be the next logical step." When you speak up for yourself you are sending a message that you have boundaries. The person taking your idea may be betting on the fact that you are going to remain silent. Set a boundary so a pattern doesn't emerge where you no longer want to share your great ideas.

Depending on the context, you can approach the person to discuss what is happening privately. He/she may be taking them unintentionally, but by having a conversation you make them aware of their actions. Also, a company may own the rights to the ideas you generate depending on the circumstance, but you are entitled to the recognition for your contribution if that is important to you.

Keep an idea journal where you track all of your wonderful ideas on a daily basis and celebrate your creativity.

# 24

# Ask for a raise.

My client Sharon came to me for help to find the courage to ask for a raise. She had had a bad experience at her last job, where she believed that hard work alone would result in a good raise.

One day, Sharon's co-worker and friend Tina, told Sharon that she had asked for a significant raise and received it. Tina enlisted the help of one of the senior members of the company to advocate for her because she had done market research and realized she was being underpaid. She encouraged Sharon to ask for the same raise since they performed the same job at the company. Sharon's response was "That's so nice for you. I can wait for my annual review in a few months." Sharon believed that she would be given the identical raise and wouldn't need to justify her work or do any due diligence. When Sharon had her review, she was given glowing remarks about her good work. However, she was given significantly less money than her friend Tina. She was confused and upset but didn't say anything.

Sharon learned a hard lesson that seemed counter intuitive. She was disappointed that being a dedicated employee, and going the extra mile didn't translate into the same raise as her co-worker who was doing the same job. She assumed that she would be awarded the same amount as her peer and didn't need to do more.

Through our work together, Sharon was able to learn from her previous experience. She realized that her colleague did due diligence on the market and also knew that having an advocate within the company could support her securing the money she felt entitled to earning. Sharon also realized the importance of taking action when someone gives you key information about what you could earn. It isn't enough to work hard and trust that you will be rewarded.

Sharon was able to prepare for and feel comfortable asking for a raise at her current job. She did research to make sure that she was asking for the amount that the market warranted. She prepared a list of her accomplishments so she could highlight the specific contributions she had made to the company. Sharon secured the raise she deserved and within a few years, was earning six figures. Sharon had now learned how to properly ask for a raise.

The truth is that often, the people who self-promote, generally get recognition, praise and better raises. Ask for the raise you deserve.

**DESIGN A LIFE YOU LOVE CHALLENGE**
If you feel that it is time for a raise:

1. Write a list of your accomplishments and make them very specific. Keep an ongoing list throughout the year. A manager will be able to do more with the facts. For example, be clear about how you saved the company money or impacted the bottom line.

2. Find out what others are getting paid for the same job at your company or at competing companies. The more due diligence you do in advance, the better. It is important to present the data factually versus as a threat. You are just providing facts to show that you care enough about your job to do it well, and want to be paid what the market dictates.

3. Practice what you are going to say, don't just wing it. Ask someone qualified to role-play with you. Look at yourself in a mirror and pay attention to your body language and what messages you are conveying. Do you look confident or afraid? How is the tone of your voice? Do whatever you can in advance of the meeting to be prepared so that you can boost your level of confidence. Also, dress professionally to show that you take yourself and your work seriously.

Don't be discouraged if you don't get the raise. There are many reasons that a company may not be able or willing to meet your request. It is an important skill to learn and one that will empower you.

# 25

## Don't wait for others to validate your work to know it is good.

So many women and men work hard and wait for another person to validate their efforts. Often they work harder and longer in the hope of hearing some recognition of their good work and contributions. However, in business, what often happens, is that it is the people that promote themselves that get recognition. It is important for you to know your worth and work in a way that honors your time without the need for external validation. Although you deserve to be recognized for your efforts, it is just as important that you know the value of your contributions.

If you have dreams that you want others to tell you are worth pursuing, you could wait a lifetime. People don't always understand the vision you have for something. Trust that you know what is right for you. Don't wait for permission or acknowledgment to have the courage to take action on your dreams!

**DESIGN A LIFE YOU LOVE CHALLENGE**
Create a list of the value that you have brought to your company so you don't forget. Keep adding to it as you produce more for your place of employment, or if you are an entrepreneur, for your clients and customers. This is a way of recognizing your accomplishments.

As the list grows, so will your belief in your good work. Take pride and ownership in your work so that you are in a position of confidence when it comes to advocating for yourself for a raise, promotion or even a new job. Do something nice for yourself to celebrate your achievements.

# 26

## Take pride in your work, no matter how big or small the job or task.

So many people are in jobs that they don't enjoy. It is a hard situation to be in. Whether you love or hate your job, what you produce at work is a reflection of you. When you take pride in your work, you feel better about yourself. It boosts your confidence and makes you feel more in control.

Since you have to be at work for many hours, you owe it to yourself to make the most of that time, so that you can feel good about yourself. Always do your best even if you aren't in your ideal position. You never know who may notice your positive, "can-do" attitude, and give you an opportunity you never would have dreamed possible. You also get the satisfaction of knowing you did your best. Use the time to gain new skills and qualifications.

**DESIGN A LIFE YOU LOVE CHALLENGE**
Journal using the following questions as prompts:
If you don't enjoy your work, how can you still bring the best of you to your job? What can you do to make it more enjoyable for yourself? How would it feel if you accepted your job for the moment and gave your best to honor yourself? What new skills can you learn?

Take pride in how you may be supporting the bigger picture goals in your life. Perhaps the work you do supports your family or is paying for your education.

# *27*

## Take control of your finances.

Having a healthy relationship with money is essential to your well-being. It allows you freedom. It means that you don't have to rely on anyone for what you need and desire.

If you have never been taught about managing money, you can learn. There are books, resources on the web, and classes offered at local education centers. If you have someone in your life who is proven at managing money, then they can be a resource for you as well.

Generally speaking, the basic rules are: pay yourself first so you have savings; pay bills in full to avoid credit card debt; don't buy things you can't afford; create an emergency fund that would cover your expenses for at least three months, and enjoy your money on fun things if you can afford it. It also helps to understand the inherent value of things, which puts into perspective what is worth paying more for and what isn't.

Many married couples approach money in a very traditional way where all assets are merged. Regardless of whether you decide to combine finances, in addition to a joint account, make sure to have an account solely in your name. The idea is that you don't need to ask your partner for funds for everything you want to purchase. You aren't left in a position where you have to justify every purchase you make. Create a system that allows for some freedom and autonomy.

**DESIGN A LIFE YOU LOVE CHALLENGE**

1. Make sure you have a checking and savings account in your name.

2. Take some time to understand your relationship with money. Write the answers to the following questions in your journal. Do you have savings? Do you have debt? If so, what is your plan to pay it off? Do you rely on someone else for your financial stability? How would it impact your life if that support were taken away? Are you earning what you are worth? If not, why? What is your plan to be financially secure? Are you investing your money? Pay attention to the areas you where you need more information, resources and education.

3. Write down all of the beliefs you have about money. For example, "I am not good with money." Or something positive like, "I easily afford all that I need and desire." How can you begin to change any negative beliefs about money?

4. Take time to learn about money management if you aren't confident with how to do it. Talk to a financial advisor to make sure that your finances are set-up properly and working towards your retirement goals. Take a class on money management at a local center for adult education. Determine what other steps you can implement to become more financially savvy. Make sure that you are prepared in case of a death, divorce or other situation. Do what it takes to own your financial freedom!

*Chapter Four*

# Body

# 28

## Breathe.

Our breath is our lifeline. Some of us lose a connection to our breath and hold it in or take shallow breaths. When we are stressed out or scared, we don't allow our breath to flow properly.

From the ages of ten to sixteen, I had to wear a back brace for scoliosis 23 hours a day. It started at my neck and dug all the way down to my upper thighs. Sleeping in it was very uncomfortable to say the least. It was meant to fit so tight that I could hardly breathe. As a developing girl, the brace did its job containing the curves in my spine, but it took away my ability to connect with my body in a vital way. To this day, I find myself forgetting to breathe because I really couldn't take in a full breath for those six years.

How about you? Do you hold your breath? Do you breathe life in fully? Do you feel relaxed or tense most of the time? Maybe you had experiences that impacted your connection to your breath.

Have you ever watched a newborn breathe? They take in oxygen from their bellies, the way we were intended to. Singers know this, as they have to breathe properly to sing well. They breathe through their diaphragms, not their chests, as we often do. Over time, we develop bad habits and forget to breathe this way.

Our breath is so critical to our overall well-being because when we breathe properly it helps our body to stay grounded and to feel relaxed.

## DESIGN A LIFE YOU LOVE CHALLENGE

Whenever you are feeling stressed out or realize you are not breathing in fully, stop whatever you are doing, sit up straight and take at least three slow breaths in from your nose and exhale slowly from your mouth. The exhale should be longer than the inhale. This elicits the relaxation response which calms your nervous system. This practice is especially helpful if you tend to be anxious or often find yourself on "high alert," even when you are in a situation that isn't actually threatening.

A few simple ways to incorporate this exercise is to focus on deep breathing when you wake up and before going to bed. You can also put a reminder note on your computer to stop and breathe throughout the day so you can allow yourself to relax.

# *29*

# Cultivate a daily meditation practice.

What is meditation? My dictionary defines it as "directing one's attention toward a symbol, sound, thought, or breath to alter the state of consciousness to attain a state of relaxation and stress relief; used for spiritual growth, healing, deepening concentration, and unlocking creativity." This definition clearly articulates several benefits of meditation, and there are many more, including creating greater focus and inner peace. Many articles describe how some of the most successful people in business make meditation a part of their daily practice.

For those who have never meditated, or have tried and don't know how to do it "right," it can feel overwhelming.

**DESIGN A LIFE YOU LOVE CHALLENGE**
Here are some ideas to begin a meditation practice:
Set aside just 5 minutes to meditate every morning when you get up or before going to bed. Set a timer and position yourself comfortably by either sitting up straight in a chair or lying down (if you don't think you will fall asleep). Take some deep breaths to relax your body and mind. As you focus on your breath, thoughts will flow into your mind. Just notice them. Try to quiet your mind as best as you can by bringing your attention back to your breath. Pay attention to how you feel.

As you get comfortable with a practice you can choose to add more time to meditate. You can also research the various ways of meditating, including methods like Transcendental Meditation or Mindfulness Meditation. The key is to find what works for your schedule and what feels good to you. Meditation is to benefit your overall well-being so it should be a pleasurable experience.

There are now many apps available to help you begin or maintain a meditation practice. You can easily search for the most popular recommendations to see what works best for you.

# *30*

## Honor your body
## and it will support you in return.

Many of us take our body for granted, but it is talking to us all of the time. We may have aches, pains, stiffness or feel tired every day, and the list can go on. More often than not, we ignore the signals and don't take the time to care for ourselves.

Our minds tend to take over and we keep busy so we don't have to pay attention. We have things to do, and slowing down is not usually high on the list of priorities. The truth is by befriending your body and the messages it's trying to send to you, the more you will be able to do in the long term. Our bodies carry us through life and deserve love, respect and care.

### Design a Life You Love Challenge
Take a quiet moment and breathe deeply a few times to relax and tune into your body. Start from the top of your

head and work down to your toes as you slowly check into all parts of your body. Really connect to every part of you.

Do you clench your teeth? Is there tension in your jaw? How about your neck? How does it feel? Pay attention as you make your way down to your toes. What are you aware of? Are there parts of your body that hurt? Breathe into those areas while sending love.

Get a journal and write down any thoughts that come to mind as you scan your body. It may feel odd at first to think about talking with your body, but if you take the time to listen, you will find that it may have some specific information it wants to give you. Try to do this exercise once a week or more often if you have chronic pain or tension.

Treat yourself to bodywork that you enjoy, like massage or acupuncture. Schedule your annual physical and get your blood work checked so you can stay on top of your health. Make getting a good night's rest a priority. Sleep is vital to a healthy body and mind.

# 31

## Eat healthy. Good health is vital to living a happy life.

Hippocrates said "let food be thy medicine and medicine be thy food." By giving your body whole foods you are fueling your cells, as your body knows what to do with those foods. It isn't about eating "perfectly" all of the time, but making the best choices for most meals.

With the hundreds of diets out there, sadly what to eat has become very confusing. Some diets work for some people but not others because of something called bio-individuality, which means that there is no one right diet that works for everyone all of the time. It is why it is essential for you to pay attention to how food makes you feel. Brain fog, tiredness, bloating, gas or skin irritations are a few signs of potential food intolerance or sensitivity. The more awareness you have around how you feel based on what you eat, will help determine which foods make you feel strong, healthy and energized. The better you feel the more you will be motivated to eat well.

In addition to what you eat, make meals enjoyable. Eating can be enjoyed in solitude or with friends and family. Enjoy the sense of community that comes from sharing a meal.

**DESIGN A LIFE YOU LOVE CHALLENGE**
Here is a simple way to approach eating healthy every day:

1. Focus on eating whole foods.

2. Reduce or eliminate processed foods and sugar.

3. Keep yourself hydrated with water.

4. Add in more fruits and vegetables.

5. Choose healthy sources of protein.

6. Eat whole grains.

In addition to knowing what to eat, it requires organization and planning. It's easy to make poor food choices when you are hungry, especially if you are in a hurry. If planning in advance is not your strength, it can still be something that you manage. The idea is to keep it simple. Pick one meal, like breakfast, and write down ideas for the week, including meals that you could prepare in advance that would allow for healthier options.

Once you get into a routine with breakfast, move on to lunch, snacks, and dinner.

If you need extra help, hire a personal chef, health coach or ask a good friend who enjoys cooking to help you with meal planning, and ways of preparing and storing the food in advance. Check your local grocery store, as many now offer free or affordable cooking classes and recipes on their websites. You can also check the web for useful resources or look for an "app" that can address this. Many people choose to prepare their food on the weekend, usually on Sunday, with a trip to the grocery store in the morning, but you need to schedule how you do it in a way that works for you and your family.

# 32

## Move your body every day.

Our children are our best teachers. As you watch a child, you see them constant in motion. They stretch, twist, twirl, dance, hop, climb, play, and leap. We know deep down that we are meant to move but as we get older, many of us lose that motivation to exercise our bodies regularly.

So, how do you reconnect with your body in a way that feels good to you? First, it is important to listen to your body and what kind of movement makes it feel energized. There are so many options—like walking, dancing, tai chi, yoga, swimming, and cycling—among many others. Think about times in your life when you were active and what activities made you feel great. If your friends like to run but when you do, your knees hurt, or you feel exhausted afterward, then that is not likely the type of movement you will want to do. Do you love to dance?

Maybe you feel best after a yoga class? For others, it's something more intense like a spin class that really gets you fired up.

**DESIGN A LIFE YOU LOVE CHALLENGE**
Here are three ways to incorporate and commit to moving your body every day:

1. Before you begin, write down your big picture goal on a sticky note. For example, "My goal is to become stronger so I have more energy to play with my children." Or "My goal is to de-stress through exercise for a better quality of life." Put the note on your refrigerator, on your mirror, in your bathroom, by your bed or wherever it is going to be seen to motivate you. By connecting to the big picture of why you want to exercise, it reminds you why it is important to keep this commitment to yourself.

2. Ask a friend who is also interested in the same type of exercise to buddy up with you for accountability. Pick one to three days a week at the beginning where you meet up to exercise. Be realistic with your schedule so you set yourself up for success. We are more likely to show up when we have someone else counting on us.

3. Make movement a fun part of your day and not a chore. Take a long walk with a friend. Have walking meetings. Take the stairs more often. On

a nice day, get off the metro a stop early or walk to work. Sign up for a dance class with your partner or dance with your kids. Hula hoop! Register for a team sport. Pick something that you truly enjoy, and you will be more likely to commit to it.

# 33

## Love and accept your body as it is in this moment.

Very young girls love their bodies. They admire themselves in the mirror with curiosity. There is no judgment, just love. Sadly as girls enter elementary school and get a little older, their awareness of their body starts to shift. External images, magazines, comments from adults and other sources start to create a negative framework for many girls about how their body should look to be acceptable. It is heartbreaking to see a young girl who no longer loves her body. That same young girl may grow into a woman who now hates what she sees in the mirror. How can we reclaim our love for our body? It is important first to accept it and love it as it is.

Learn to embrace all parts of yourself—the parts that you love—and the parts that you wish were different. Even more important than how you look on the outside, is how you feel about yourself on the inside. It is those feelings that generate your level of confidence and your ability to attract genuine love. When we are fully in our bodies, embodying who we are, that is when we truly shine. It's coming from a much deeper place than the superficial realities that are imposed upon us women in this world. We dictate what is beautiful by loving ourselves as we are.

In the United States we are obsessed with certain ideals of beauty. However, anytime you are fixated on changing how you look to please others, you abandon yourself. If you have bought into the idea that you need to have large breasts, a small waist and thighs and a button nose, that doesn't serve your higher purpose on this planet. You deserve love, respect and admiration just as you are now, and forever. Start loving your body and yourself today.

**DESIGN A LIFE YOU LOVE CHALLENGE**
Look at your body in the mirror with the curiosity of a little girl. Suspend all judgment. Do you see that your body is worthy of your appreciation? What parts of your body do you criticize? Why? What parts of you do you wish were different? Why? What parts of your body do you like? Pay attention to how you feel when you give yourself positive feedback. Give your body loving messages instead of criticism.

Think back to what messages you received or continue to receive that make you think your body is not okay as it is. What would these parts say if they had a voice? You can choose to love and accept those parts as they are.

Write your body a love letter and express gratitude to every part of it, even the parts that you don't like. Thank every part of your body for all that it does for you every day.

# Chapter Five

# Relationships

# Focus on being genuine, not perfect.

In the fast-paced world in which we live, many people try to paint a perfect picture of themselves. They act differently than how they really feel. True joy comes from being able to show your genuine self. Your genuine self is the most authentic expression of who you really are.

From the time that we are very young, we are taught how to think and behave. All of those different messages that come from parents, teachers, friends and relatives may erode that connection with our true self. As you get older, those influences in your life and your temperament will impact how much of you remains intact.

The good news is that the real you that was so strongly in her body when she was born is still there and yearns to have a voice. If you have found that you have lost your connection to that beautiful voice of yours, you can always retrieve it anytime by being true to yourself.

We've all had experiences with someone who expresses herself in a way that makes you feel connected. The recognition of that person's authenticity inspires a desire of our own expression. So how do you get there?

**DESIGN A LIFE YOU LOVE CHALLENGE**
Take time to connect with the real you. Journal using this prompt, "The real me is." Next, write down all of the things that made you feel happy and alive as a child. What games did you like to play? What activities did you like to do? How would you spend your free time? The answers to these questions connect you with that part of yourself that knows just who you are.

Once you have more awareness about what makes you happy, like if you used to love to act, sing, draw, or dance, find ways to incorporate those activities into your life. Don't compromise who you are to please others. Make a practice of bringing your authentic self into all of your relationships.

# 35

## Forgiveness is the foundation for peace, love and good health in your life. Learn to forgive yourself and others.

There are people in your life who may hurt you or push your buttons. It is easy to get caught up in the anger or resentment, but ultimately that just robs you of time and emotional energy that could be spent enjoying life.

You don't have to forget what was done to you or keep those who have hurt you close, but by forgiving them you are freeing yourself from those negative bonds.

We have all had times when we have done things we wish we could go back and do differently. Punishing yourself isn't going to heal the past, and it keeps you stuck in pain.

**DESIGN A LIFE YOU LOVE CHALLENGE**
Write a list of the people that you need to forgive. Think about how you can forgive each of them in any way that would feel good to you. Perhaps you want to write a letter so you have an opportunity to express your feelings and then discard it, as this exercise is to benefit you. Or when you are alone, you can think of the person in your mind and express out loud what you want to say to them.

Sometimes we are better at forgiving others than we are at forgiving ourselves. We are human and make mistakes, so forgive yourself as well for any pain that you have caused. Now that you have new awareness, you can ensure that those situations do not repeat themselves in the future.

# 36

Every person in our life is a mirror of a
part of us.  Some parts we admire,
and other parts we don't.
All relationships are a gift.

A re there people in your life who you were drawn
to the moment you met them?  And others who
drive you crazy?  We often see the relationships
that feel good as the ones that are beneficial to our
development, but even the relationships that cause pain
provide an opportunity for us to learn and to grow as
individuals.  This is not to say that somebody who has
hurt you should remain in your life.  It is however an
opportunity for you to see the areas that you have belief
systems in, and to shift those beliefs.  For example, if
you tend to be a people pleaser, you may attract others
who rely on you to take care of them.  It also becomes an
opportunity to set healthy boundaries with others.  The
more we surround ourselves with people who make us
feel happy, the better our lives will be.

## DESIGN A LIFE YOU LOVE CHALLENGE

Make a list of the people closest to you and write down the three attributes that best describes them. For example, is the person kind, generous or funny? How about confident, controlling or outspoken? What are the qualities that they possess that attracted you to them in the first place? What are the qualities you admire and the ones you resent? Is it possible that what attracted you to them is your need to develop those traits within yourself? By having a better understanding of each relationship you can use it as a road map to embody the attributes you need as well as have compassion for the qualities that you would like to work on. It is also an opportunity to assess your relationships to determine how much time you want to invest in them moving forward.

# 37

# Bring your full self into the relationship. Don't compromise on the things that bring you joy.

Ann loved to dance and did so regularly. She took competitive ballroom dance classes for many years. She felt alive and happy when she danced. After she got married, she slowly gave up dancing. Instead, she would do the things that her husband liked to do. He didn't like dancing and was clear about that boundary, but she encouraged his hobbies and chose to let go of her own. During our work together, she realized that she didn't have to give up something she loved because he didn't want to do it with her. She began taking dance classes again. When her husband saw her commitment to herself and how happy she was, he even agreed to go dancing with her every once in a while! It was her passion for her own interests that drew him to her in the first place.

Do you cater to your partner, husband, family or friends without thinking about what you really want? Do you find yourself compromising on things that are important to you? Do you feel safe expressing what is bothering you and that you will be supported?

It can take time to learn how to fully show up in relationships so that we can be seen and have our needs met. It takes practice to speak up in the moment or take action without feeling the need to ask for permission.

**Design a Life You Love Challenge**
Think about your relationships. In which ones do you compromise your desires to please the other person? Why do you do that? Write down a clear description of how you would like the relationship to be. What needs to change? Do you believe it is okay to speak up for yourself? Are you honest about your feelings? If not, why?

What activities/hobbies can you incorporate back into your life to bring you pleasure?

# 38

## It is okay to limit or end relationships with people that drain your energy.

Do you have people in your life who, after you spend time with them, leave you feeling exhausted and "less than?" When we are young, we often accept those relationships as part of our reality. However, as we get older, we learn that these relationships are toxic and not okay for our well-being.

There are some relationships that we are locked into, such as with relatives, but that doesn't mean you can't set healthy boundaries. It is okay to honor yourself enough to limit the amount of time that you spend with them. Your truth is your truth, and if someone is draining you, you need to be your own advocate.

Life is a precious gift and the people we surround ourselves with help make it that much more happy and meaningful. To waste time with people who drain our energy hurts us deeply on an emotional level.

## DESIGN A LIFE YOU LOVE CHALLENGE

Pay attention to how you feel when you are around your family, your friends and other significant people in your life. Do you walk away feeling wonderful or depleted? Is there a consistent pattern of a lack of boundaries? In those cases, you need to decide whether this is someone who needs to be in your life. If not, then limit or eliminate the time you spend with them.

If it is someone that you can't avoid being around, then you need to be proactive about how to minimize your exposure to their negativity. Plan in advance how you will handle the familiar but unwanted violations to your personal space by doing things that will help you cope. For example, find time to be alone so you can recharge, even if it is for a moment. Remind yourself that even if it feels personal, it isn't about you but a reflection of the other person's issues.

# *39*

## Genuine friendships do exist. Don't settle for anything but true connections.

We all have a desire to belong, and to be a part of a community. At different times in our life, making connections is easier than at other times. We may forego our true self to please others and to fit in. However, real joy and satisfaction come from being able to be your genuine self and be accepted for who you are as you are. You deserve to be loved for the things that make you unique. It is okay to consciously spend time with someone who you don't fully click with, but the people that you want in your "inner" circle of friends are the genuine souls that you can trust with your vulnerability.

Women may wear their heart on their sleeves, giving the best of themselves to everyone, to only then be betrayed by people they thought were their good friends. Just because you may be kind and loving towards everyone doesn't mean that is how all people will be towards you. Limit the time spent with negative people. It isn't about being friends with everyone, but being able to have a smaller group of people who share your values and the love you have for yourself.

**DESIGN A LIFE YOU LOVE CHALLENGE**
Assess your friends. Do you have genuine friends that you enjoy being around and spend time with regularly? If not, take the time to cultivate close relationships. Just like with your husband, boyfriend or partner, the time with these people shouldn't feel like work. It should lighten your heart and make you feel at home. Your feelings are the barometer you want to look at when determining whether someone is worthy of your time.

# If he says he loves you but his actions are contrary, then move on and live your life. Find someone who can make the commitment you deserve.

Many of us have dated someone who we adored who didn't treat us the way we deserved. He says "I love you" but treats you counter to those words. You can waste too much time on someone wishing that he would change. Remember that you can only control how you behave. You can't change someone else.

Actions do speak louder than words in relationships. What we learn with experience is that a person who acts counter to the sweet nothings isn't worthy of our love and time. When you are in love with yourself and treat yourself like the goddess you are, you won't settle for anything less from your significant other.

By understanding your values and what you need out of your relationship, you are able to discern what you require in a partner to enjoy a true partnership. Knowing what you want out of a relationship guides who you will—and will not—commit to.

**DESIGN A LIFE YOU LOVE CHALLENGE**
Questions to journal about:
- Are you in a relationship that makes you feel loved and honored?

- Are you happy more often than sad when you are together?

- Do you feel excited to be with him?

- Does he love you as you are or does he try to change or control you? Does he treat you with respect and care?

- Is his temperament consistent or are you on an emotional roller coaster?

Treat yourself the way you want to be treated in the relationship. If he is able to value you as you are, that is great. If not, don't settle. It is up to you to set the tone for how you are treated and to set boundaries that honor you. Physical or emotional abuse is never okay.

*41*

# Model what you want your children to learn. They do what we do, not what we say.

As a mother, I am more aware of how my actions are creating a strong impression on how my daughter will be in relationship to others and herself. Our children, both boys and girls, are looking to us parents as their role models and mentors. We are guiding their path with not just what we tell them is important, but more significantly by how we behave. Yes, our children are born with their own temperaments but we are shaping the way they value themselves.

**DESIGN A LIFE YOU LOVE CHALLENGE**
Journal about the following:
What did your parents model for you? How does that impact who you are in the world today? Did you follow their lead or do you parent differently because you didn't like what was modeled for you?

What are you modeling for your children? Are you your full self or are you stuck playing a role in your family structure? Is there anything you would like to change?

By being true to who we are, we empower our children, heal the legacy of our ancestors who struggled so much for us, and raise the consciousness of what is possible for everyone around us.

# Make "giving" a priority.

We live in an interconnected world. Everything we do impacts other people. When we make a conscious choice to give of ourselves in a positive way, we can help those around us.

There are many ways to give and the way that you choose should feel natural to you. Giving doesn't have to involve money; it can be your time, knowledge or resources.

**DESIGN A LIFE YOU LOVE CHALLENGE**
Are you interested in doing more to help others? Here are some suggested ways to give of yourself starting today:

1. Smile. Smiling at others is one of the simplest and easiest ways of giving that can have an uplifting impact on people. For one day, experiment with smiling at everyone you come into contact with— even smile at the people walking down the street.

2. Time. Pick a non-profit or school that needs help and commit to giving your time for a specific project or a regular commitment. If you want to help children, start there. If the idea of helping the elderly excites you, then begin at an organization that helps older people.

3. Donate money. There are so many charities that need financial aid. Find one whose mission you believe in, and make a one-time or ongoing donation.

4. Give someone a compliment. This is a nice way of connecting with others in a genuine way. Tell a teacher what a great job she is doing. Thank the person who delivers the mail to your home for their hard work.

Keep the idea of giving front of mind. You will find that it not only makes others feel good but that it brings you happiness as well.

*Chapter Six*

# Simplicity

# Simplify your life.

Do you wake up feeling like your day is already planned and you have no control over your time? Do you have so many balls up in the air, that you don't know how you will manage to get it all done? Are you so tired at the end of the day that you fall asleep the moment your head hits the pillow—or worse—you can't sleep at all because so much is going through your mind?

You deserve peace of mind. Life is meant to be enjoyed. It isn't a sprint; it is a journey. So how do you regain control of your life when things feel out of control? How do you make time to do the things that are most important to you?

**DESIGN A LIFE YOU LOVE CHALLENGE**
Simplify your life by taking stock of what is and is not working. For the areas that require simplifying, review a typical week, and assess what commitments you

don't need or have time to do yourself. Make a list of those things and then revisit the exercises in inspiration #5, which focuses on priorities. Decide what routines would make your life easier and begin implementing those habits.

Remember that you are in control of the thoughts you think and the actions you take. You can simplify any situation in the moment by staying present and taking a step back from the situation to evaluate your next step. For example, if your current habit is to check your phone for new messages the moment you get out of bed in the morning, you can choose to stretch your body instead or do whatever will help set a positive tone for your day.

*44*

# De-clutter your life.
# Make room for what you desire.

How do you feel when you walk into your home? Your office? Your bedroom? How about your kitchen? Is it organized and calming or filled with clutter and weighing you down?

On an emotional level, clutter drains your energy. Everywhere you look there are things that distract you. There are items that need a place to be stored, which means more work for you, and the mind is unable to relax. If you have children it can be even tougher to maintain a clutter-free home. The reason that people often don't begin de-cluttering is that it feels overwhelming.

When we take time to get rid of the things that we no longer use, need, or want—we make space for new things, situations and opportunities to come into our lives. We create a peaceful environment, which allows us to relax.

**DESIGN A LIFE YOU LOVE CHALLENGE**
Make a list of each room in your home that needs some organization. Write down specifically what you want to accomplish in order to get that space the way you desire. This includes whether you need to purchase filing cabinets for an office or pull together all of clothing you haven't worn in years for donation. Keep it manageable. Every week, pick one area to de-clutter. You can start small like with a drawer, or if you feel motivated, the entire bureau, but give yourself permission to just do that one thing so that you feel motivated to begin. If you have more time to commit to the project, spend an hour a day until the room you want to work on is done.

Pay attention to how you feel once the space has been cleared out. Are you more relaxed? Is it easier to get dressed in the morning? Do you have more time in your day because you aren't searching for specific items anymore? Once you experience how good it feels, it will keep you moving forward.

If you need additional help or assistance, there are many resources online as well as books that you can review to help you de-clutter. You may also consider outsourcing the project if it is too much to do on your own.

# Be Authentic.

This is a simple statement but really profound. Authenticity is at the heart of living your truth and allowing for meaningful connections with others. When we pretend to be someone we are not, we die a little inside because your soul wants you to remember who you are and to express it in the unique way that only you know how. There is a beautiful book called, *"The Art of the Snowflake: A Photographic Album"* by Kenneth Libbrecht. When snow falls, collectively, it is so pretty, and each flake appears to be ordinary. However, when you see the photos in the book, you see that every flake is extraordinary and no two are the same! It is so inspiring and it is just like every precious life on this planet. Even if you feel like you have nothing special about you, deep down you know the truth. You carry a special gift that only you can bring to this planet for its well-being. Celebrate what makes you unique.

**DESIGN A LIFE YOU LOVE CHALLENGE**
Use your journal to explore more about the real you. Think about any area(s) in your life where you don't feel like you are being your authentic self. Whatever you are feeling, know that it is okay.

Here are some questions you can use when you journal: "Why am I not fully showing up and expressing the real me? Am I afraid of rejection? Of not fitting in? How would it feel to show the real me? Am I willing to be more visible the next time? Who am I?"

# *46*

## Pick a theme song that lifts your spirits.

Music is so powerful. It evokes many different emotions depending on the genre we choose. Do you have a favorite song? A song that when played makes you feel uplifted?

There may be times when you wake up not feeling yourself or just need to shift out of the energy you are experiencing. Music is a powerful way to change how you feel or to express yourself.

**DESIGN A LIFE YOU LOVE CHALLENGE**
Find a song that makes you feel great every time you hear it. Dance and sing along to it alone or with the people around you. Here are some other ways to use music to bring you joy:

1. Have the song cued up to play when you wake up in the morning or to help you feel energized.

2. Play your favorite upbeat song and sing along while you are in the shower.

3. Make a list of the songs that you love the most and create a playlist on your phone so you can easily access it when you need a lift.

4. Schedule regular dance breaks during the day for a quick energy boost or when you are feeling down.

Let the power of music feed your soul.

# Make serenity a priority.

The definition of serenity is "The state of being calm, peaceful, and untroubled." How often do you find yourself in a state of serenity? When we experience it, it feels so good, but it requires awareness and discipline to achieve.

We are constantly taking in information through various forms—emails, tweets, texts, television, radio, podcasts, conferences, Facebook, Twitter, Instagram, Snapchat, Pinterest, Google plus—and all of the next ways of communicating through social media. One of the challenges that we face with any form of communication is that so much of it, especially when it is related to the news, is intended to generate fear. It is fear that makes us no longer want to take risks. It is fear that keeps us stuck and unable to make decisions. It is fear that creates ignorance that fosters violence. Even with all of the social media, we are not connecting on a soulful level that allows for much meaning. These forms of communication become a distraction, and we risk losing a connection to what is really important in life.

## DESIGN A LIFE YOU LOVE CHALLENGE

Be mindful of how often you take in information and connect with others. Make a pact to turn off your cell phone, even for just an hour when you are visiting with family or friends, or after you pick up your children from school. During the day, limit your time with technology to two or three designated times so you aren't reacting to what is coming at you. Turn off all devices (phone, laptops, and ipads) by 8pm every night and don't check them until the morning.

Write a list of what makes you feel peaceful and incorporate more of those activities into your life. Create a morning and/or evening ritual that allows you time to feel calm and peaceful. For example, light a candle, read an inspirational quote, go for a walk, focus on what you are thankful for, play soothing music, take a bath, watch the sunset, or hug someone you love. Schedule time every day to experience serenity.

# 48

## Surround yourself with beauty.

According to the *Merriam-Webster* dictionary, the definition of beauty is "the qualities in a person or a thing that give pleasure to the senses or the mind."

Beauty is subjective, which makes it that much more interesting. One person can adore a painting and another will not like it at all. What is so great about beauty is that we can easily surround ourselves with things that are pleasing to our mind and senses. When we do that, we feel more relaxed, happier and inspired.

**DESIGN A LIFE YOU LOVE CHALLENGE**
Think about the ways that you can bring more beauty into your life. Perhaps it is by surrounding yourself with the little things that can make you feel happy—like a fun, cool pen to write with and an accompanying journal. Maybe it's fresh flowers that you purchase for your-

self every week. Perhaps a pretty scarf or lip-gloss in a beautiful color makes you feel good. Create or purchase a beautiful piece of art. Take a walk in a garden or on the beach. Add beauty to your life every day to bring in inspiration and joy.

# 49

# Dress like the Goddess you are!

How do you feel when it is time to get dressed? Do you love the clothes and accessories you have? Do you enjoy getting dressed in the morning? Do you feel feminine and beautiful? Do you feel put together and confident? Did you have a time when you felt good about what you wore, but let that go after getting married or having children? Did you have a certain style that no longer works for you now that you are older, and you aren't sure how you want to present yourself?

You deserve to feel your best every day. The clothes you wear should be an expression of you and make you feel great. Women can make excuses why they shouldn't buy something they love, but wouldn't think twice about getting something more expensive for their partners, husbands or children.

Would you like to reclaim some of that passion for putting yourself together in a way that makes you feel happy and confident? You deserve it!

**DESIGN A LIFE YOU LOVE CHALLENGE**

1. Look through Pinterest, fashion magazines, fashion blogs, or whatever outlet is fun for you and get a sense of what styles you like.

2. Write a list of the basics you need and some fun items you would like to add to your wardrobe.

3. Go through your clothes, including accessories, and assess every item you own. If you feel beautiful when you put it on, keep it. If there are items you haven't worn in a year or never wore, it is time to donate them or give them to a friend who would enjoy wearing them. If you have a friend who needs to do the same thing, plan on taking turns helping each other clearing out the items. Keep it fun.

4. Once you have cleaned out your closet, it is time to shop! Many stores have free personal shopper services if time is an issue or you don't like to shop.

5. You don't need many clothes; you need clothes that you enjoy wearing—and the basics that can be mixed and matched. The 80/20 rule applies here—most of us wear 20 percent of our clothes,

80 percent of the time. That is why there are so many items just sitting around collecting dust. Let them go and get your goddess on!

# 50

## Relish in the little things.

When life gets too busy or is stressful, we can always turn to the little pleasures in life to revive our spirit. These little things bring fresh inspiration and hope. They make us feel alive and remind us of life's pleasures.

In "*The Prophet*" author Kahlil Gibran writes, "For in the dew of little things the heart finds its morning and is refreshed." What are the little things that bring you joy? A morning coffee with a good friend? Reading a fashion magazine? Taking a walk in nature? Enjoying a cup of tea at a café all by yourself? A hug from your child? Taking a bath? Looking at a piece of art? A kiss from your love? The list can go on and on.

Our culture makes many people feel that they need to be very wealthy or own lots of expensive things to be happy, but the truth is that we have so much abundance all around us in the little things.

**DESIGN A LIFE YOU LOVE CHALLENGE**

Take time to think about and write a list of the little things that bring you joy. How can you incorporate and appreciate one item from your list every day?

# 51

## Practice the art of gratitude.

We all have many things to be grateful for, but we're often striving for the next goal or have obstacles that leave us feeling down. The act of being grateful attracts more good into your life and sets the stage to attract the things you desire. There is something that happens on an energetic level where like attracts like, so when your energy is focused on the good, you attract more good. No matter what is happening in your life, there is always something you can be grateful for, even if it doesn't feel that way in the moment.

**DESIGN A LIFE YOU LOVE CHALLENGE**
Make a daily practice of being grateful and keeping a gratitude journal. Every morning and/or evening write down at least three things that make you feel grateful. Being grateful doesn't need to be just about big things. It can be the love you feel when holding your child's hand or the joy of drinking your morning coffee. By writing

them down, it helps you see all of the wonderful things in your life.  Keep it simple and see how it shifts your energy for the better!

# 52

## We live in an abundant world.

D o you believe there is enough for you? Enough time, money, love, resources, or whatever you need and desire? Do you act from a place of abundance or do you see other people's successes as a threat to your own?

When you can trust that there is enough for everyone, you can relax and focus on your unique contributions in this life. You may have an idea and realize that many others are already doing or expressing the work that you want to do. Remind yourself that it is okay because you have your own unique way of doing and saying things that will resonate with people who aren't able to receive it from the others. You don't have to compete with others. You just need to get into action and focus on what you want to do.

The CEO of a major corporation used to tell me that he never looked at what the competitors were doing. He kept his focus on what he envisioned as possible, and put all of his energy into making it a reality. His belief that there was always enough business led to his incredible success and financial abundance.

## DESIGN A LIFE YOU LOVE CHALLENGE

Write down the areas in your life where you feel abundant. It is good to appreciate and see how it exists for you. Then write down the areas where you have belief systems that make you feel that there isn't enough. How can you change those beliefs to the positive? Try turning each negative belief into a positive affirmation. Instead of thinking, "There are already too many artists."—tell yourself—"My art is unique and many people will appreciate it." Embrace the abundance that exists in the world.

# Conclusion

I hope that this book inspires you in many ways. I kept the format simple to encourage you to find the time to think more about your life. I also wanted to make it easy for you as you explore each concept.

Life is to be enjoyed. When life is running us—versus us being in charge of who, what and when we spend our precious time—we compromise our ability to fully experience the best it has to offer.

Invite your friends to go through the 52 weekly exercises with you. You will find that by doing it in a community, it brings a sense of closeness with yourself and others. It also becomes an opportunity to go deeper and to learn from the experiences of other women.

There are too many women (and young girls) who live in cultures that do not allow them to have their voice and express their gifts. We are very fortunate in the United States to be able to pursue what makes us happy. By being your full self and expressing that in this world, you not only lift yourself but all of your fellow sisters on this planet.

May you live with joy, love, inspiration, great health, supportive relationships and simple pleasures.

With love and gratitude for you!

*Michele*

# Acknowledgments

Thanks to my amazing parents, Mona and Robert, who have always instilled within me a desire to help others. Every day you lead by example what it means to practice unconditional love, kindness, and dedication to family. To my brothers Russ and Bob, I'm so grateful for your love, friendship, and how you make me laugh. Thanks to all of my amazing family and friends who bring love, support and joy into my life daily.

My deepest gratitude goes to—Alexandra Abbott, Amy Driscoll, Kristen Noonan, and Rodney Raftery—who took the time to read the book before it was published and provide valuable feedback. Thanks to Bruce Jones who encouraged me to keep writing and for being the ideal accountability partner—and to Joshua Rosenthal for inspiring his students to go for their dreams. A special note of recognition goes to my wonderful clients for agreeing to let me share their experiences so that others may be inspired by their journeys.

To my amazing husband and daughter—thank you for your never-ending love and support. I love you with all of my heart!

# About the Author

Michele Lamoureux is a lifestyle coach, writer and speaker. She hosts a weekly podcast for women called "The Good Life Coach" filled with practical and actionable tips to live a happier, successful and more fulfilled life.

Michele spent 15 years working in corporate America as an international marketing director before becoming a certified life and holistic health coach, with the desire to empower women to design a life they love. As an empowerment coach, Michele helps women find their voice and the courage to pursue what matters most to them. Michele offers corporate trainings, workshops and individual coaching to help women live with greater purpose and joy.

22171383R00074